PRACTICAL LANGUAGE TEACHING

Editors: Marion Geddes and Gill Sturtridge

No. 4

The Magazine Picture Library

PRACTICAL LANGUAGE TEACHING
Editors: Marion Geddes and Gill Sturtridge

The Magazine Picture Library

JANET McALPIN

London
GEORGE ALLEN & UNWIN
Boston   Sydney

First published in 1980

GEORGE ALLEN & UNWIN LTD
40 Museum Street, London WC1A 1LU

© George Allen & Unwin (Publishers) Ltd, 1980

British Library Cataloguing in Publication Data

McAlpin, Janet
    The magazine picture library.—(Practical
    language teaching; no. 4).
    1. English language—Study and teaching
    —Foreign students 2. English language—
    Study and teaching—Audio-visual aids
    3. Illustrated periodicals in education
    I. Title II. Series
    428'.2'4078   PE1128.A2

    ISBN 0-04-371061-1

Typeset in 10 on 12 point Times by Trade Linotype Ltd, Birmingham
and printed in Great Britain
by Hazell, Watson & Viney Ltd, Aylesbury, Bucks

Contents

Acknowledgements

I wish to acknowledge my debt to my predecessors and contemporaries at the British Council's English Language Teaching Institute in London, where the magazine picture library was conceived and developed with imagination and enthusiastic co-operation.

I would also like to thank the following people for permission to use advertisements and photographs:

Times Newspapers Ltd
Rowntree McIntosh & Co.
Guardian Royal Exchange Co.
General Accident
Colt International Ltd
Costain Homes
Phillip Morris Ltd
Dewar's Distillery Ltd
Lyons & Co. Ltd
Corocraft Ltd
Central Office of Information
Mumms Champagne Ltd
John Scott
Diamond Trading Co.
Daks-Simpson
Dunlop Footwear Ltd
Johnnie Walker
Citroen Cars Ltd
Dutch Marketing Board
British Tourist Authority
Peter Combes

1 *The Value of a Magazine Picture Library*

The magazine picture library can provide a low cost and versatile teaching resource for the language classroom. The aim of this book is to suggest how teachers or groups of teachers might select, prepare, store and use such pictures. The initial step is to establish a small library, classified in a simple way, so that pictures are easily found when they are needed, and easily replaced after use. The advantages of the library will then become clear: teachers will have ready access to a range of pictures which, with a little imagination, can be used to enrich their lessons in a variety of ways.

1.1 WHY MAGAZINE PICTURES?

Magazines are a source of coloured illustrations and advertisements, many of which are ideal visual aids.

1.1.1 CHEAP AND EASY TO FIND

Since the pictures need not be recent, any source of discarded magazines will do. You may collect old issues from family and friends, from the waiting rooms of obliging doctors and dentists, from libraries or from embassies. Some markets have stalls for secondhand publications. Magazines will be the main source of pictures for your library, but there are other sources. Free pamphlets, brochures and catalogues contain pictures, so don't throw these away when they fall into your letterbox. Pictures from old calendars, postcards and greetings cards are often worth saving. Once you have developed an eye for useful teaching pictures you will find them in all sorts of unlikely places—even the gift wrap round your birthday present!

1.1.2   A VARIETY OF PICTURES

Different types of magazine will provide different types of picture. Women's magazines contain information about such topics as cooking, fashion, famous people and home decoration, and therefore are a source of pictures of food, clothes, famous faces, furniture, kitchen implements and various household objects. Hobby magazines have pictures of special equipment, and sometimes action shots. Nature magazines have pictures of animals, plants and outdoor scenes. Travel brochures will provide pictures of famous places and monuments, beach and mountain scenes, restaurant interiors, and hotels.

Magazine pictures are usually authentic and colourful. Some are illustrations of articles. Others are advertisements. Most of them are photographs, as clear and attractive as the publisher can print them. For this reason magazines are a rich source of pictures that would be hard to collect from any other source. It is impossible to draw, for example, the kind of mouth-watering roast chicken that appears in food advertisements, or the kind of exciting action shot that might appear in a sports magazine after the World Cup. This kind of realism is appealing to students as a change from other visual aids such as simple chalkboard drawings or stylised published wallcharts.

Moreover, magazines often contain pictures which are imaginative or unexpected. Picture 1, for example, is from an advertisement for a national newspaper. It shows a disappearing hand holding a paintbrush which has not quite finished painting the notice DANGER, QUICK SAND 20 YDS. This picture was accompanied by the subtle caption '*Have you ever wished you were better informed?*' to form a clever advertisement for *The Times*. Without the caption it is a perfect classroom picture—a big, clear and realistic representation of an intriguing situation. This sort of picture is a gift from the advertiser to the teacher, as it is full of potential for the classroom.

1.1.3 A VARIETY OF USES

Pictures can be used as an alternative to chalkboard drawings to present new situations or vocabulary items. They can be used as flashcards, to cue substitution items in oral drills. They can be used as wallcharts are used, to stimulate oral or written composition, or to prompt discussion.

Pictures can also be given to students to use in pairs or groups, for practising structures or vocabulary. Certain pictures are suitable for making games or puzzles. Later we will look at specific ways in which magazine pictures can be used not only at different stages of the lesson, but also for different activities.

1.2   WHY A LIBRARY?

There are several advantages to organising your collection of pictures into a simple library.

1.2.1 A SOURCE OF READY PICTURES

A library of magazine pictures, carefully classified, provides a source of pictures to which the teacher can refer when he needs a specific illustration. He might be looking, for example, for pictures to illustrate new vocabulary in a lesson—a television set, a rainy day, or a wedding. He might be looking for pictures which clearly show the difference between countable and uncountable items. He might be looking for a picture to illustrate a verb such as *eat,* or two pictures to illustrate a tense contrast, such as *is eating* and *has eaten.* The library will probably contain all these pictures, thus saving him the trouble of drawing them or searching for them elsewhere.

1.2.2   A SOURCE OF IDEAS

On the other hand, a teacher who has no particular idea in mind might simply browse through the library looking for inspiration. Pictures can suggest their own exploitation. A teacher who knows his class needs further practice with the present perfect tense might come across Picture 1 in the library and immediately see its potential for some excellent classroom practice. This picture will elicit:

> *He is painting the notice. He has painted nearly all of it.*
> *He is sinking into the sand. He has sunk almost completely.*
> *He is disappearing. He has not disappeared completely.*

Five minutes' work with the picture could add an extra sparkle to this teacher's next lesson.

1.2.3   ACCESSIBILITY TO ALL

The same picture might be useful in different lessons for different purposes. For example, food pictures might be used in one lesson to teach food vocabulary, and in a later lesson to prompt changes in a pattern such as:

$$There \begin{cases} \textit{aren't many xs.} \\ \textit{isn't much y.} \end{cases}$$

Pictures can also be used at different levels. A beginners' class might simply guess the meaning of *quick sand* and learn the word *danger* from Picture 1. An intermediate class might discuss why the situation has occurred, practising sentences using *because*, or predict what will happen next, practising the use of *will* or *going to*. An advanced class might plan and roleplay an official enquiry into the loss of the signpainter.

Putting a picture into the library multiplies its usefulness by making it available for different purposes to teachers of all levels.

2 Building the Library

In this chapter we discuss how to select, prepare, classify and store magazine pictures.

2.1 HOW TO CHOOSE PICTURES

In starting a magazine picture library the essential aim is to build up a corpus of good pictures. You may not know exactly what you will do with each picture in the classroom, but this is not important. Indeed, if you select pictures only on the basis of the lessons you are teaching this month, you risk rejecting pictures that will prove unexpectedly useful next month. The important principles of selection do not, therefore, lie in your immediate recognition of a teachable structure or vocabulary item represented in the picture, but in the quality of the picture itself. Is it large or small? Is it bold and clear? Is it unambiguous?

2.1.1 LARGE PICTURES

Large pictures will be shown to the whole class, and must therefore be big enough to be seen by all the students. Magazine pictures are ideal for use with classes of fifteen to twenty; in larger classes it will be necessary to show the picture separately to sections of the class. The size of your class will influence your decision about selection of a picture, depending on how quickly you think the students will see and grasp its content.

Exposure of a picture should be fairly brief, to keep up the pace of the lesson. Therefore the visual information in it should be readily understood. Time will be lost if the picture has to be passed to every member of the class, so you should consider not only the size of the picture but also the clarity. A small, simple picture of a sandwich might be perfectly suitable, while a large, detailed picture of a banquet may puzzle the students if they cannot decipher it from the back of the room. A badly printed picture will be unsuitable. A cluttered picture will be distracting. An ambiguous picture will be unhelpful if the students cannot decide precisely what it shows.

In other words, if a student cannot see what is in the picture, if he cannot decide which part of it you want him to look at, or if he cannot tell what the picture is supposed to represent, then the picture is unsuitable: the students will be too preoccupied with peering at the picture to respond promptly in the way you hoped they would. You should therefore reject any picture which is blurred, cluttered or confusing. Good pictures which are too small to be seen by the whole class need not be rejected, however, but can be put aside for a box of small pictures which can be used for groupwork.

2.1.2 SMALL PICTURES

In groupwork or pairwork, pictures will be examined more closely by the students, so the size is not important. Clarity is still essential, however, since the objective is to stimulate language related to a recognisable object or action. Any picture which confuses you will probably confuse your students, so unless you want them to discuss these confusions it is better to discard blurred or ambiguous pictures.

Groupwork is usually a time for practising new language. It is therefore useful to have small pictures which reproduce items already familiar from a previous presentation by the teacher. Small pictures of objects, places, animals and people are as useful as large pictures, if they are used for follow-up practice. (These pictures can frequently be found in catalogues and brochures.) Small pictures of simple actions, such as a girl typing, children playing with toys, or a man fishing, are also useful.

Since it is important to have enough pictures for several groups or pairs of students, duplicates will be necessary, so do not discard another small picture of a chair or a hotel because you already have one. Your collection of small pictures must be big and extensive if it is to be useful—there will be an opportunity to discard unnecessary pictures later, when your collection has grown with constant additions.

2.1.3 PICTURES FOR GAMES AND WORKCARDS

Certain pictures, large and small, are suitable for communication games to be played by the whole class or by pairs of students. Some of these pictures will be included in your general collection; two games which utilise such pictures are described in Chapter 6. Other pictures can be specially prepared on cards or in folders to form a small student-access library for pair practice or individual work. The following is a general guide to the selection of pictures for this purpose.

Curious pictures, such as Picture 1, can be collected for a game called *Describe and Draw*, in which one student tries to describe the picture accurately enough for his partner to draw a rough replica. Pictures useful for this game are those which show familiar objects in an unusual arrangement, or strange shapes which make a describable pattern.

Identical pictures, usually from duplicate copies of one magazine, can be collected for two other games. In *Describe and Arrange*, one student has a complete picture, such as the clocks in Picture 2, and his partner has the same picture in jigsaw parts. The first student must tell his partner how to arrange his picture to match the model. In *Identify the Pair*, one student has a number of similar pictures, such as the photos in Picture 3, and his partner has a duplicate of one of them. The student must ask his partner questions until he can establish which of his pictures is identical with his partner's. This game can also be made when you find just two matching pictures—the set can be completed from other sources.

A fourth game can be made from similar, but not identical pictures, such as the hands in Picture 4. In this game, *Find the Differences*, the two students must ask each other questions until they can find a specified number of discrepancies between their pictures.

In this type of game the pictures act not only as a stimulus, but also as a communication check.[1] After performing the task, the students can compare their pictures and discuss the reason for any mistakes they have made.

Pictures with plenty of detail, or which show an interesting situation, can be made into workcards for individual work. Picture 5, for example, could be pasted on a card with the following exercise written below:

TRUE OR FALSE?

1. *The egg is in the middle.*
2. *The newspaper is on the plate.*
3. *The spoon is on the plate.*
4. *The flowers are in the eggcup.*
5. *The toast is beside the flowers.*
6. *The squirrel is on the left of the toast.*

Alternatively, a simple story called A SURPRISE FOR BREAKFAST could be written beneath this picture to make a reading text, or a guided composition task could be prepared by leaving gaps in the story for students to complete, or by making a list of questions which will help the students to write the story in their own words.

The preparation of this type of work is time-consuming, but it is worthwhile if it leads to a substantial collection of activities to occupy your students. So do consider all the possible uses of a picture before you discard it. In fact it is useful, when you begin your magazine picture collection, to prepare separate folders marked LARGE, SMALL, GAMES, READING CARDS, COMPOSITION etc., so that the pictures you find can be immediately allocated to the right one.

2.2 HOW TO PREPARE PICTURES

A certain amount of 'scissors and paste' preparation is necessary to ensure that your pictures can be handled easily and often with minimum damage. If you work with co-operative colleagues you will find that occasional picture preparation sessions are an enjoyable staff activity. Alternatively, if you teach children you may be able to enlist their enthusiastic help. For a good session you need plenty of table space, magazines, scissors, card, pens and time—perhaps a scheduled meeting. A guillotine is a help, and labelled folders will serve to store the pictures you have to leave unmounted for the next session.

2.2.1 TRIMMING

Pictures may come in odd shapes, and if they are advertisements they will carry a caption. This caption will be a distraction to the students—they will crane to read the words while you are trying to focus their attention on the picture. Cut off the words or, if they intrude into the picture, camouflage them with a coloured pen to match the background. Trim the picture to a convenient shape. Picture 6 shows how a useful picture of horses can be obtained from an advertisement for cigarettes.

2.2.2 MOUNTING

Teachers or teaching departments with money to spend may buy card for this special purpose, but it is not important that all the pictures be mounted on card of the same size, colour or quality. The important thing is to glue the pictures on to something stiffer than paper to make them more durable and to prevent the light from shining through when you hold them up in class. So cost-conscious teachers are advised to save *any* card for this purpose: old folders, files, boxes, shirt stiffeners or stocking packaging will do. Since card is difficult to cut with scissors, a guillotine is a help if you have one, but it is not essential.

2.2.3 LAMINATION

Teachers with access to lamination paper may wish to cover the pictures in order to preserve them from frequent handling. While this is desirable for popular pictures, in practice there are some drawbacks. Pictures can become obscured slightly when covered with shiny plastic. Moreover, lamination is expensive, and wasted on rarely-used pictures, and it is not always possible to predict which pictures will prove the most useful. However, you may make a guess and laminate the pictures you think will be most popular, or those you know will be handled by students. An alternative is to have a set of plastic folders in the library to slip the chosen pictures into for classroom use. Otherwise, just take care to glue the edges of the picture securely and to leave an extra rim of card, as it is usually the edges of a picture that tear. Never laminate the back of a picture—this should be left as a writing surface for noting the code and teachers' comments.

2.2.4 CODE

The simplest way of noting the classification code of the picture is to write it on the back of the picture. This precaution will make it easy for each teacher to replace the picture where he found it. The type of code used might be a number, a word or a letter, depending on your classification system. Keep the code simple and consistent, write it boldly in a corner of the card on the reverse side of the picture, and make sure all borrowers know how to use it.

2.3 HOW TO CLASSIFY

Whether pictures are to form a private collection or a staff collection, the secret to forming a useful library lies in their classification. Pictures must be easy to locate when they are needed, and easy to replace after use.

2.3.1 CLASSIFICATION BY SYLLABUS

Many teachers have favourite pictures to use with certain lessons. Perhaps these pictures illustrate new vocabulary items which appear in that lesson, or perhaps they depict some aspect of a situation which is used to contextualise a teaching point. Similarly you may, when selecting pictures, be able to predict the precise point on your syllabus when a picture will prove useful. Picture 7, for example, would clearly be useful when you are teaching the present perfect tense:

> *Someone has dented his car.*
> *Someone has backed into his car.*

In these cases the temptation is to classify the pictures according to when you plan to use them. If this is according to the lessons of your coursebook, Picture 7 might be classified as 'Lesson 15: Picture 1', or '15.1.' If you classify according to your syllabus it might become 'Present Perfect: Picture 1'.

These two approaches to classification presuppose that a teacher knows exactly what he will use a picture for when he selects it, but this is not always the case. It also presupposes that each picture will be used for one purpose only, and this is wasteful. It would be a pity to lose the opportunity to use Picture 7 on another occasion to practise the verbal constructions:

> *He's going to be late.*
> *He was going to drive away but now he can't.*
> *He must be amazed.*
> *It wouldn't have happened if he had arrived a moment earlier.*

An alternative, and in fact simpler, classification system makes it possible to build a library of pictures without predicting precisely how they will be used. In this system, pictures are classified according to their content, thus allowing the pictures to be more versatile and the teachers to exercise more imagination in their personal choices.

2.3.2 CLASSIFICATION BY CONTENT

Magazine pictures can be broadly divided into two simple categories: things and people.

Things are usually static—a bowl of fruit, a gold watch, a gleaming new car, a football. This category of static things might be extended to include living things such as an oak tree, a dog, a garden scene, or even a face wearing spectacles or modelling a hat. From this sort of picture you can elicit not only names of things and their parts, but also the language of size, shape, colour, number, location, properties, comparison etc. You will find it difficult, however, to elicit the language of action, since none is represented, or the language of time, since this sort of picture is timeless, with no forward or backward reference.

Pictures showing people may be static, as a passport photograph is static, showing only expressionless facial features, or as a portrait is static, showing identifying characteristics which might include a symbol of occupation, such as a uniform or musical instrument. This sort of picture can also be used to elicit names and adjectives.

Most 'people' pictures, however, are not static. They show some sort of animate behaviour: a boy eating an apple, a woman presenting a gold watch to a man, a family picnicking beside a car, a footballer scoring a goal. With these pictures we can ask what is happening, and how, and why, and when, and what is going to happen next. They show activity, and therefore are related to a moment in time. With these pictures you will be able to elicit tenses and time phrases, as well as statements of cause and effect, or probability, or attitude, or opinion, etc.

The two broad categories 'things' and 'people' can be divided into more useful categories, according to the type of picture that is usually found in magazines. Thus 'things' might be divided into FOOD AND DRINK, OBJECTS, TRANSPORT, HOBBIES, PLANTS AND ANIMALS, BUILDINGS and perhaps PLACES. 'People' might be divided into PEOPLE, SPORT, ACTIVITIES and SITUATIONS. Any of these categories could be changed, or further sub-divided. For example, you may wish to differentiate between pictures that show familiar situations, such as a driver changing a wheel, unusual situations as in Picture 1, and situations that are internationally recognisable, such as the inauguration of a president. These new categories could then be called SITUATIONS, UNUSUAL SITUATIONS and INTERNATIONAL EVENTS. You may wish to differentiate between ordinary people, famous people and people whose occupation is evident, and call these PEOPLE, FAMOUS NAMES and OCCUPATIONS.

None of these categories will be mutually exclusive, you will find, and this will cause occasional difficulties when you are classifying pictures. A football might be considered appropriate for the category SPORT; on the other hand it is an OBJECT. Similarly a footballer receiving a trophy might be classified as SPORT, or it might be considered a SITUATION. You might be unsure whether to classify a busy street as a SITUATION or a PLACE; in this case your decision will probably depend on how clearly the picture shows specific activity in the street. At these moments of indecision it is helpful to consult a colleague. The problem, however, is not really serious. Once you have made your decision you will mark the picture with the appropriate code, and thereafter borrowers will always return the picture to that category whether they agree with your classification or not. Moreover, borrowers quickly become aware of this kind of overlap between categories, and will learn to consult, for example, the SPORT file when they are looking for certain types of SITUATION picture.

2.3.3 ALPHABETICAL CLASSIFICATION

The following list of categories is one which has been used successfully to account for most of those mentioned above. The names of the categories have been chosen with a letter-code system in mind. The advantage of this system is that since the name of each category starts with a different letter of the alphabet, it is necessary to write only A, B, C etc. on the back of each card to indicate where it belongs.

There are fourteen categories in this particular system: ANIMALS AND PLANTS, BUILDINGS, CURIOSITIES, EVERYDAY ACTIVITIES, FOOD AND DRINK, INTER-

NATIONAL NEWS, JOBS, LOCATIONS, NAMES, OBJECTS, PEOPLE, RECREATIONS, SITUATIONS and TRANSPORT.

A: Animals and Plants. Pictures such as the horses in Picture 6 are suitable for this category. It contains pictures of wild and domestic animals, and of trees, plants and flowers. Teaching the names of animals and plants is not the only purpose to which these pictures can be put. A leopard, for example, is *spotted*, while a zebra is *striped*. One student may *like* roses while another may *prefer* daisies. For this reason it is useful to collect more than one picture of each species. With these you will be able to compare such aspects as colour, size and number. In Picture 6 the horses *are running*; with a picture of one horse you might introduce the singular form *is running*. A picture of a standing horse, such as Picture 8, might then be used to introduce the negative form *is not running*.

Not all pictures showing animals and plants will be best filed in this category, however. The horse in Picture 8 is being sheltered from the rain by an umbrella held by a gloved hand: this would be more appropriately classified as a SITUATION. Pictures of fruit and vegetables, while technically plants, will in most cases be more usefully filed as FOOD. The basket of fruit in Picture 9, however, belongs in yet another category. It is clearly a gift, and is therefore best considered as an OBJECT.

B: Buildings. In this category you can collect pictures of different types of building: towering skyscrapers and simple sheds, modern banks and ancient ruins, Gothic cathedrals and village churches, factories and public monuments and residences of all kinds, including palaces, villas, tenements, cottages, even grass huts and igloos. With these pictures you will be able to prompt comparative and superlative forms of such adjectives as *big*, *small*, *old*, *new*, *modern*, *primitive*, *historic*, *ugly*, *attractive*, *comfortable*, *isolated*, *well-situated*, *well-designed*, *well-constructed*. Pictures of residences might be used as aids in a house-hunting context to practise forms of polite request such as:

I'm afraid that one is too...; could you please show me something $\left\{ \begin{array}{l} \text{more} \\ \text{less} \end{array} \right\}$ *...?*

or forms of polite disagreement such as:

> *Yes, I agree that it's..., but I think perhaps it's a little too... for my taste.*

You may wish to include in this category pictures of famous buildings which your students will be able to recognise and name. Photographs of buildings such as the Tower of London or the Taj Mahal (often found in tourism advertisements or calendars) can be used to prompt simple statements such as:

> *It's the Taj Mahal. It's in India.*

or questions such as:

> *Would you like to visit India?*
> *Have you ever seen the Taj Mahal?*

C: Curiosities. This category is extremely useful for the occasional oddity one finds in certain clever advertisements, or in reproductions of modern art. Picture 10 is an advertisement for coffee. One part of the picture shows a normal cup, which could be cut out for filing under OBJECTS, or perhaps FOOD AND DRINK. The other part shows a fantasy—half a cup of coffee indeed! This picture could be an amusing aid in a restaurant context to prompt the complaint:

> *Excuse me, waiter. This is only half a cup of coffee!*

It could also prove useful in a dialogue to practise the contrast between dogmatic and less dogmatic intonation patterns:

> *Is it possible to cut a cup of coffee in half?*
> *Of course it's not possible.*
> *Are you sure? Look at this.*
> *Oh! Well, perhaps it's possible...*

Picture 11 is an example of another kind of CURIOSITY—the type that cannot be named, and therefore has to be described in terms of its appearance, or its components, or its use. These pictures can elicit language such as the responses in the following dialogue:

> *What does it look like?*
> *It looks like a tree.*
> *What is it made of?*
> *It's made of jewellery.*
> *What is it used for?*
> *I don't suppose it's used for anything, really.*

Though small, the CURIOSITIES file will grow gradually, and will prove valuable on occasions when you wish to surprise, amuse, puzzle or challenge your students.

E: Everyday Activities. This will probably be one of your biggest categories. It includes pictures of people engaged in familiar activities such as eating, drinking, smoking, reading, writing, typing, bathing, brushing teeth, combing hair, answering the telephone, posting letters, shopping, cooking, gardening, ... and such pictures are easy to collect. Picture 12 is an example of a simple, explicit picture of a very common daily activity—tying shoelaces. Picture 13 shows a boy eating a banana. Such pictures will elicit the present continuous form of the verbs illustrated if we ask *What is he doing?* However if we change the question we can practise other things as well. With a picture of a man reading a newspaper in bed, for example, we can ask not only *What is he doing?* but also:

> *What does he do every Sunday morning?*
> *What did he do last Sunday morning?*
> *What will he do next Sunday morning?*
> *What would he be doing if it were Sunday morning now?*

Picture 14 shows another common activity—talking on the telephone. However, it is important to make a distinction between the categories EVERYDAY ACTIVITIES and SITUATIONS. This girl has clearly been interrupted while bathing, and seems pleased about it. Perhaps this is not such an everyday activity after all, and should be filed under SITUATIONS.

F: Food and Drink. This category will also be large, as the pictures are both useful and easy to find. Magazines are full of advertisements for the food industry, showing pictures of flawless fruits, fresh vegetables, plump chickens, succulent meats, ripe cheeses, creamy cakes—this file will always make you hungry! The food may be raw or cooked. It may be piled in abundance on market stalls or kitchen tables, or temptingly arranged on a plate or picnic cloth. Collect the best of these pictures, and as with ANIMALS AND PLANTS, do not reject different pictures of the same item. It is useful for students to learn the difference between *boiled, poached* and *fried* eggs. A *small* cake will contrast with a *large* cake, and a *Christmas cake* can be distinguished from a *birthday cake* or a *wedding cake.*

Apart from teaching the names of different foods, these pictures will be particularly useful guides through the complexities of count and mass nouns, and the ways we can refer to them. *One banana* looks different from *a bunch of bananas. A loaf of bread* will contrast with a *slice of bread,* and the latter can also be used to prompt *a little bread* in contrast with *a few eggs.* A dozen eggs *are too many* for one person to eat and a whole chicken *is too much.*

Similarly, you will find any number of pictures of drinks: fruit juices, soft drinks, alcoholic drinks such as wine, beer and whisky, fresh milk, and beverages such as coffee and tea. These drinks may be icy cold or steaming hot, refreshing or comforting. They may be depicted in bottles, cans, cups, glasses or even packets, and the containers may be unopened or opened, full or empty. One picture may be used to show that someone has not bought enough beer for a party: *He should've bought more.* Another picture can show that he bought too much whisky: *He needn't have bought so much.* An empty bottle will lead a student to deduce: *It has been drunk.* A full glass will prompt the negative: *It hasn't been drunk,* or the prediction: *It will be drunk.*

This category provides pictures for teaching structures as well as vocabulary, and is a source of substitution prompts for a range of shopping or restaurant situations.

I: International News. At times it is useful to have pictures of such international events as your students will recognise immediately: pictures of ceremonies such as the inauguration of President Carter, the coronation of Queen Elizabeth, or of man's first steps on the moon; pictures showing the wedding of a famous pop star, or the funeral of a pope. International disasters could be included: pictures of the survivors of the famous Andes aircrash, or of the aftermath of the last earthquake in Peking. These pictures, like some in other categories, will be useful for eliciting statements based on general knowledge, or for prompting discussion.

Structures can also be elicited from these pictures. The passive form can be illustrated by certain events:

> *The President was inaugurated.*
> *The Queen was crowned.*
> *The Space Shuttle was launched.*

Dates, whether provided by the students or the teacher, can be used to practise time phrases, or to prompt questions:

> *What happened in . . . / on . . . / during . . . ?*

They will also be useful to practise *since* and *ago*:

> *It is a year since Argentina won the World Cup.*
> *Argentina won the World Cup a year ago.*

Some of the pictures in this category will be ephemeral. Others will have meaning to some students and not to others. In order to aid your own memory in the classroom it is a good idea to note a few facts on the back of each picture before you file it in this category. These notes will help you to supplement what the students themselves know with accurate information such as precise dates and names, if necessary.

J: Jobs. Picture 15 is a photograph of a chef. Not only is he wearing the uniform of his profession, but he is also surrounded by evidence of his work—an elegant banquet, ready to be served and eaten. Pictures which clearly illustrate an occupation in this way can be usefully filed in this category. It could contain pictures of air hostesses, truck drivers, policemen, teachers, labourers, grocers, motor mechanics, teachers, hairdressers, secretaries, opera singers, waiters—any occupation, whether it can be readily named or not.

Some of these pictures will be useful for teaching the names of the more common jobs. They might also be used, at an elementary level, to contrast the present simple and the present continuous tenses:

She's a guitarist. She plays the guitar. She's playing it now.
He's a taxi-driver. He drives a taxi. He's not driving it now.

Others might be used at a more advanced level to practise stating deductions with *must*:

She's an air hostess. She must like flying.
His job is dangerous. It must be well-paid.

Others can call on the general knowledge of the students to provide information such as:

Every day she has to open the mail, answer the phone, make appointments, type letters . . . etc.

or to make speculations such as:

He probably plays in an orchestra/practises every day/ likes classical music/goes to bed late/earns a good salary.

Pictures of people engaged in jobs of a more unusual nature can elicit speculations at a more advanced linguistic level.

L: Locations. Here it is useful to have a collection of pictures which can be used to indicate 'where', rather than 'who', 'what' or 'how'. This category includes outdoor scenes depicting city or country, beaches, riversides and mountains, streets and gardens, snow scenes or deserts. Interior locations are also useful: kitchens, bedrooms, dining rooms, restaurants, classrooms, shops, offices, railway carriages, airports. These pictures could be used to prompt contrasts with *but*:

> *He likes the city but she prefers the country.*
> *He spent his holiday at the beach but she spent hers in the mountains.*

They might also be used to prompt question forms in the present perfect tense. In the following situation something is lost, and students ask:

> *Have you looked in the bedroom?*
> *Have you checked in the bathroom?*
> *Have you left it in your office?*

Some pictures are symbolic of places that have proper names—towns, cities and countries. Picture 16 could clearly be used to connote Britain, England or London, and is suitable for inclusion in LOCATIONS to prompt such prepositional phrases as *in London, to London, from London, near London,* or time clauses such as *While he was in England . . .* or questions such as *Have you ever been to Britain?*

These pictures, like pictures of famous buildings, can be found in tourism advertisements and calendars. Picture postcards are usually too small for general classroom use, but they are an excellent source of LOCATION pictures for your groupwork file.

N: Names. This category is rather like the INTERNATIONAL NEWS category in that it contains pictures which will be particularly useful for eliciting language based on general knowledge and opinion. NAMES is the category for portraits of people who will be recognised by your students. Picture 17 belongs here. So do pictures of well-known political and historical figures, stars of sport, screen and pop music, famous musicians and artists, famous writers and scientists, even fictional characters such as Mickey Mouse.

O: Objects. Perhaps one of the largest categories, this may at some future stage need to be subdivided into equipment, clothes, furnishings, etc., but initially you should put all these pictures into the one file. Any picture which shows something inanimate can be included here: radios and record-players, razors, knives, cups and plates, shirts and shoes, pens and watches, typewriters and books, beds and chairs, candles, mink coats and diamond necklaces . . . the list could be endless. The clocks in Picture 2 could be filed in OBJECTS; so could the basket of fruit in Picture 9, 'the normal' coffee cup from Picture 10 and the pair of baby's booties in Picture 18. Such pictures can be used to provide substitution items in any number of language practice situations—to make a shopping list, or a list of gifts, or a list of things stolen in a burglary, or of things one would buy if one had the money.

With OBJECTS you can compare colour, number, size, function, and characteristics. You can match objects with owners from PEOPLE. You can convey such concepts as comfort, cost, or age: the booties in Picture 18 are clearly very *new,* very *clean,* and *tiny,* in comparison, say, with a pair of men's boots. They could also be used as the first in a sequence of footwear chosen to elicit *when he was a baby* as opposed to *when he was a child/a teenager/an adult/an old man.*

Pictures may show several objects: clothes in a cupboard, or plates and glasses on a shelf. These can be used to elicit the language of location. The objects on the table in Picture 5, for example, can be described in terms of their relation to each other:

> *The egg is in the eggcup.*
> *The spoon is beside the eggcup on the plate.*
> *The flowers are between the squirrel and the toast.*

P: People. This is a useful category for those pictures of people who are not engaged in any particular activity or situation (in which case they would probably belong in EVERYDAY ACTIVITIES or SITUATIONS) and whose occupation is not evident (in which case they would belong in JOBS). These are pictures of all kinds of people with which you will elicit vocabulary such as *old, young, smiling, frowning, fat, thin, rich, poor, calm, worried, fair, dark, delicate, strong, well-dressed, over-dressed* and so on. You might compare these people to elicit these adjectives. You might use them to elicit defining clauses such as *the girl who is wearing glasses ..., the man who is standing under the tree....* They might be used to practise sentences with stative verbs such as *He looks..., He seems..., He appears to be....*

You might, alternatively, use a picture from PEOPLE to establish the appearance of a character you want to introduce in a classroom dialogue, or you might ask the students to match a selection of people with possessions from OBJECTS, houses from BUILDINGS, and cars from TRANSPORT.

One of the most common characters on the pages of magazines is the professional fashion model, such as the man in Picture 19. It is not easy, however, to find many suitable PEOPLE pictures of this kind: models are usually photographed in most unlikely poses, with little expression on their faces. Once you have collected a few examples of elegant men and women, smiling and serious, you will find that you have exhausted their possibilities. Pictures of the old, the fat, the ugly, the poor, and pictures of people with something interesting about their expressions, will be more likely to be found in advertisements for products other than clothes, and in photographs which illustrate magazine articles.

R: Recreation. This is the category for pictures related to sport, hobbies and entertainment. Some of these will overlap with other categories—a pop star photographed in action on stage may be considered for JOBS, or NAMES, or even possibly LOCATIONS. The decision will probably depend on how well-known he is, and whether he dominates the picture, or is merely part of a general concert scene. This category is for pictures which refer to recreational activities, rather than to particular personalities. It will therefore contain pictures of people picnicking, fishing, playing golf, watching a football match, listening to music, skating, diving and swimming, skiing, dancing, motor racing, or attending a ballet class.

You will not always know whether a picture shows a hobby or a profession—a man surrounded by stuffed birds may be an amateur collector, or a professional taxidermist. However, hobbies can also be illustrated by inanimate things: the clocks in Picture 2 could be used to signify clock-collecting. Similarly, pictures representing sport and entertainment need not necessarily show the activity itself. The sports equipment in Picture 20 clearly connotes tennis.

S: Situations. Since ordinary situations have been allocated to EVERYDAY ACTIVITIES this category is for those pictures which show something a little more unusual. It requires more than just the naming of parts to describe these pictures. Picture 4 does, for example, show a pair of hands, first without handcuffs and then with, but it also shows that the man has been arrested, and immediately one wants to ask 'Why?'. Picture 8 shows a horse, an umbrella, and a gloved hand, but again one's curiosity regarding the reasons is aroused. Under what circumstances would this happen? Why is the horse so special? In Picture 14, the girl in her bathtowel is not looking at all disconcerted at having had to run, wet from her bath, to answer the phone. Why? Who is she talking to? All these pictures contain elements which can prompt the students to make conjectures about the circumstances.

A situation such as the one shown in Picture 14 also has backward and forward reference. That is to say, the students can be asked to tell what happened before the picture was taken (*She was taking a bath; the phone rang; she probably jumped out of the bath and grabbed a towel...*) and what will happen next (*She will eventually hang up, return to the bathroom, finish drying her hair, get dressed...*).

Sometimes the implications in a picture are very subtle. Picture 21 shows a wedding party. The groom is beaming, and the bride is looking devotedly at him. The groom's family also looks cheerful, but there are certain tensions among the bride's family. A closer look will reveal subtle differences of dress and demeanour that hint at a class difference between the two families. It is this, perhaps, that is causing the family on the left to look askance at the family on the right. This sort of analysis could be made in class, and could lead to conjectures about how it happened. Did the groom marry his boss's daughter? And how might relations between the families continue?

Picture 22, like the hands in Picture 4, shows a story in two parts, but a rather surprising one. Initially the picture could be used to practise *outside* and *inside,* or *try* and *succeed,* or the meaning of *to attempt the impossible.* The picture might, however, be used to prompt an amusing response in a dialogue such as:

Could you please answer the telephone for me?
I'm sorry, I'm in the middle of putting the elephant in the car.

Picture 23 shows some cheese and a painting, yet something strange is happening. The figure in the painting is eating the cheese! This is a most unusual situation indeed, and should be filed in SITUATIONS even if you have no immediate idea how to exploit it. If it is in the file, it will one day prove to be exactly what you need.

T: Transport. This is the final category in this system, and it needs little explanation. Here you will file pictures of cars of all shapes, sizes, colours and types, including family cars, sports cars, and racing cars, modest cars and expensive cars, brand new cars and battered old cars. You will also file pictures of planes, trains, buses, liners, yachts, ferries, hydrofoils, canoes . . . and don't forget the humbler forms of transport such as the donkeys in Picture 24.

2.3.4   POSSIBLE MODIFICATIONS

The alphabetical code and the categories described above have proved both simple and efficient in an institute where a dozen teachers used the magazine picture library daily. It may, of course, be modified to suit your purposes. You may wish to change, add or subdivide categories. You may even wish to translate the category names. If, for example, you teach in a non-English speaking country, and there are teachers of other foreign languages in your department or institute who wish to make use of the picture library, then names in your mother tongue might be more appropriate.

The alphabetical code system can also be extended. If your filing system is appropriate, you may give each picture a number, such as A1, A2 etc., in order to be able to refer to specific pictures in lesson notes or in a list of teaching aids for different stages of your course. In this case, a card index is a helpful repository for teachers' suggestions. In the section for each lesson, teachers can note the numbers of pictures they found particularly useful, with brief explanations about how they were exploited. Numbering pictures is, however, a more complicated and time-consuming procedure; a simpler system for sharing ideas is suggested in Chapter 3.

2.4 HOW TO STORE

Storage is always determined by available space and storage facilities, therefore the following are merely suggestions. The important thing to keep in mind is accessibility—no teaching resources should be stored so inconveniently that difficult access discourages busy teachers from using it often.

2.4.1 LARGE PICTURES

In the initial stages your collection of pictures will be small, and folders will be adequate for storing them. Later you may wish to transfer the pictures to file drawers, or boxes. It is advisable to store the pictures near a convenient working surface, so that teachers have somewhere to put the pictures as they browse through them.

2.4.2 SMALL PICTURES

Ideally these should all be glued on to a filing card of standard size, and kept in a filing box with dividers labelled with the categories. A more ambitious scheme is to prepare some cards with two different items, such as a girl on the left and a school on the right, or a man on the left and an aeroplane on the right. These cards are intended to prompt students to make connections, and can be filed under that name.

2.4.3 GAMES AND WORKCARDS

Sets of pictures for games to be played by the whole class can be stored in clearly labelled folders, with details of content and procedure glued to the front for teacher reference. Games for groupwork or pairwork can be prepared in folders of a standard size, with instructions for students glued to the front, and stored in clearly labelled boxes to form sets for student access. Workcards for reading or composition practice can be similarly prepared on cards of a standard size, and stored in labelled boxes. A set of such boxes containing materials for different games and exercises will form the basis of a small library of student-access resources to which the students can help themselves during special classroom sessions or when they are waiting for their classmates to finish some set work.

3 *Using the Library*

This chapter gives some general advice about using the magazine pictures in your library. The following chapters will give detailed suggestions about classroom exploitation of various types of picture for different purposes and activities.

3.1 HOW TO SELECT PICTURES BEFORE CLASS

You may want a picture to illustrate a situation which you plan to use for presenting a new structure or tense. This type of picture will normally be found in SITUATIONS, or perhaps in EVERYDAY ACTIVITIES or INTERNATIONAL NEWS.

You may want a set of pictures to use for prompts in a substitution drill. Select these from OBJECTS, from FOOD AND DRINK, or from TRANSPORT, ANIMALS AND PLANTS, BUILDINGS, or PEOPLE. These pictures offer you the opportunity not only to practise names, but also to elicit comparative statements, so you may find it useful to select these pictures in contrasting pairs.

You may wish to use a combining technique with pairs of pictures from, for example, JOBS and LOCATIONS: *The postman lives in the city; This musician works in a restaurant;* etc.

Certain pictures will elicit statements based on general knowledge, for example pictures of famous people from NAMES, or from INTERNATIONAL NEWS.

For presentation you will need one or more illustrative pictures. For practice drills you will need sets of six or more. For groupwork or pairwork you will need sets of six or more for each group. Collect these systematically in relation to the activities you have planned for your lesson.

3.2   HOW TO HANDLE PICTURES IN CLASS

Before the class you should plan exactly which pictures you are going to use, and when, and place them in the correct order. In class you should display the pictures clearly, making sure all students can see them, and leaving time for them to digest what they see before you request a response. You will find from time to time that students interpret the picture differently from you—in this case, discuss the picture—do not insist that your interpretation is correct, but try to guide the students to see what you see. With certain pictures it is helpful to establish what they represent before you proceed to elicit the required response.

Students enjoy 'fun' pictures—an inappropriate item in a set of Christmas gifts, an inappropriate person in a gallery of party guests. Include these when appropriate, but always ensure that students realise your choice is a joke!

3.3   HOW TO SHARE IDEAS AFTER CLASS

After your class, you may wish to share your ideas, particularly those which have worked well, with your colleagues. If you have a card index you may write your suggestions there. A simpler system, however, is to write on the back of the picture the language you have elicited from the picture and the lesson you used it in. Teachers browsing through the library can then look not only at the pictures, but also at the notes on the back, which may suggest some refreshing new ideas.

4 Recognising Language in Pictures

S. Pit Corder made a useful distinction between two types of visual material. He called these 'material for talking *about*' and 'material for talking *with*.[2] This distinction can be usefully applied to the exploitation of magazine pictures. When a picture is used as an object for description or comment, the students are being asked to talk *about* it. When it is used as an accessory to a contextualised dialogue or a discussion the students are being asked to talk *with* it. This second approach can lead to language that is not suggested by the picture at first glance. To help you recognise potential language in pictures this chapter suggests four ways in which different types of language may be elicited from your students. Techniques for doing this in the classroom will then be discussed in the remaining chapters.

4.1 DESCRIPTION

At first glance, the language one readily associates with a picture is the language needed to describe its components. The names of these components—and their parts, their colour, size and shape, their location etc.—represent potential vocabulary items. If these items are placed in the context of a statement they represent potential sentence patterns. Vocabulary items and sentence patterns can be elicited by asking questions about the picture such as 'What can you see?', 'What colour is it?', 'Is it big?', 'Where is it?' or 'What is happening?'. The answers will refer to explicit features of the picture.

4.1.1 EXPLICIT VOCABULARY

At word level, the names of components and their attributes give us nouns and adjectives. Thus, in Picture 18 we might identify the nouns *booties, pair, wool, lace, ribbon, ring,* and the adjectives *blue, pink, tiny, new.* Similarly, from Picture 19 we might elicit *man, hat, suit, shirt, tie, gloves* and *tall, smart, dark-haired,* and from Picture 8 *horse, rain, umbrella, arm, sleeve, glove* and *white, wet, dry.*

Naming behaviour gives us verbs such as *walking* and *smiling* from Picture 19, and *standing, holding* and *raining* from Picture 8. Adverbs may be added to descriptions of behaviour: in Picture 13 we might say that the boy is smiling shyly and in Picture 21 the groom is certainly smiling *happily.*

Naming location or direction can elicit prepositions and prepositional phrases. We have seen how the objects on the breakfast table in Picture 5 could give us phrases such as *on the right, on the left, between, in front of, behind.* The horse in Picture 8 is *under* the umbrella, and the umbrella is *over* the horse. The man in Picture 19 is walking *towards* us.

Using pictures to illustrate isolated words or phrases such as these can be useful as a means both of teaching the meaning of vocabulary and of prompting student recall.

4.1.2 EXPLICIT STRUCTURES

As soon as we make sentences about pictures we are using structures. The obvious statement about any picture uses the present tense, either the present simple as used to describe the components of Picture 18:

> *There are two booties.*
> *They are new.*

or the present continuous, as used to describe what is happening in Picture 19:

> *The man is walking.*
> *He is wearing a suit.*

Negative forms can also be elicited. In Picture 19 the man *is not hurrying*; in Picture 17 the Queen *is not smiling*; in Picture 8 the horse *is not getting wet*.

Passive voice can be elicited from some pictures. In Picture 18 the booties *are made of wool*; in Picture 8 the horse *is being sheltered*; in Picture 9 the coffee *hasn't been drunk*; and in Picture 4 the man *has been arrested*.

Pictures can also be used to elicit statements which require agreement of number and gender. In Picture 19 the man *is walking*, while in Picture 24 the donkeys *are walking*. In Picture 19 *he* is carrying *his* gloves, while in Picture 17 *she* is wearing *her* gloves. Similarly, when practising word order it is useful to have a picture such as Picture 18 to identify the adjectives *two*, *blue* and *new* before placing these in their correct order: *two new blue booties*.

Short answers, in both affirmative and negative, can be prompted too. If we ask the question 'Can he tie his shoelaces?' about Picture 12 we will get the answer *Yes, he can*; the same question about the handcuffed man in Picture 4 would probably evoke *No, he can't*. Alternatively, we might practise longer sentence constructions by asking students to use linkers to combine statements about a picture. In Picture 14 *She is sitting on the stairs and talking on the phone*; in Picture 21 *His mother is smiling but her mother is not*; in Picture 8 *He is holding the umbrella over the horse because it is raining*. The complexity of such constructions can be increased according to the level of your class.

4.2 INTERPRETATION

All the language suggested above has been elicited by asking questions about what can be seen in the picture. We can also ask questions about what is implied in the picture.

4.2.1 IMPLICIT VOCABULARY

Pictures also convey associations. Although Picture 18 shows a pair of booties, it also conveys the idea of *baby,* or *new baby,* or even, because the booties are blue, the idea of *baby boy.* Picture 20 carries the association of *tennis* or *sport;* Picture 9 could be used to suggest *gift.* This implicit vocabulary might refer to abstract notions: with Picture 7 we might convey the idea of *anger,* with Picture 13 the idea of *hunger* and Picture 16 has associations with *London,* or *tradition,* or *tourism.* These associations extend the range of vocabulary that can be derived from a picture.

4.2.2 IMPLICIT STRUCTURES

Many pictures contain references to the immediate past. Pictures such as 4 and 22 show 'before' and 'after' explicitly: the man's hands are first free, and then handcuffed; the elephant is first outside the car, then inside. In other pictures this backward reference is implied: in Picture 14 we infer that the girl was in the bathroom when the telephone interrupted her; in Picture 21 we assume the wedding party was in church a few minutes earlier. Backward reference allows us to elicit statements using past tenses:

> *A few minutes ago he was a free man.*
> *He didn't know whether the elephant would fit in his car.*
> *While she was having a bath, the telephone rang.*

Other pictures refer to the immediate future. Thus we can infer from Pictures 12 and 20:

> *He is going to play football.*
> *He is going to play tennis.*

and from Picture 14 we can predict with reasonable certainty:

> *She will hang up, return to the bathroom, dry her hair and get dressed.*

When interpreting pictures we can also make speculations about possibilities and probabilities. Who is the girl talking to in Picture 14?

> *Perhaps it's her boyfriend.*
> *It may be her mother.*

What about the horse in Picture 8—why is it receiving such splendid treatment?

> *It might be a valuable racehorse.*
> *It could be the queen's favourite horse.*

And where is the man holding the booties in Picture 18?

> *He might be buying the booties in a shop.*
> *Probably he is in the hospital, giving them to his wife.*

Speculations can also be made about the past or the future. Why has the man in Picture 4 been arrested?

> *He might have robbed a bank.*
> *He could have hijacked a plane.*
> *Perhaps he murdered his wife.*

And what will the wedding party in Picture 21 do next?

> *They will probably go to a reception.*
> *They might drink champagne.*
> *There will probably be speeches.*
> *They may take more photographs.*

The language of explanation, prediction and speculation can be elicited by asking questions such as 'What happened or might have happened before?', 'What do you think is taking place in the picture and why?', and 'What will happen or might happen next?'

4.3 CONTEXTUALISED RESPONSES

So far, all the language we have derived from the pictures has been in response to questions about the picture itself. From these questions we have been able to elicit a wide range of vocabulary items and structural patterns. There is, however, a further range of language that can be elicited by using a different technique. Instead of asking questions about the picture, the teacher creates a context in which the picture is used to suggest an appropriate response in a dialogue.

At a simple level the context might be choosing Christmas presents for the family. Pictures 18, 20 and 9 might be used to cue the responses in the dialogue:

> *What shall we give the baby?*
> *Let's give him a pair of booties.*
> *And young Tim?*
> *Let's give him a pair of tennis shoes.*
> *What about Aunt Jane?*
> *Let's give her a basket of fruit.*

In a similar dialogue we might use the same pictures to practise a different response:

> *Would these do for the baby?*
> *Not really, he never wears booties.*
> *What about these for young Tim?*
> *Not really, he never plays tennis.*
> *Would Aunt Jane like this?*
> *Not really, she never eats fruit.*

This technique allows you to elicit language that does not seem related to the picture until it is used in a context. The following are some types of response which can be cued by pictures in this way.

4.3.1 OFFERING OR REQUESTING

Would you like some coffee?
Help yourself to a banana.
Let's have a game of tennis.
Need any help with that elephant?
May I borrow your car?
Would you mind removing that squirrel?
Could you please hold the umbrella for me for a moment?

4.3.2 ACCEPTING OR REJECTING

Thank you, I'd love { *some.* / *one.*
I'd love to but I am going to a wedding.
No thanks, I think I can manage.
I'm afraid not, it's just been dented.
I'm sorry, I can't stand squirrels.
I will if you'll take off these handcuffs.

4.3.3 STATING PREFERENCES

No thanks, I'd prefer { *a sandwich.* / *some cheese.*
He'd rather play football.
It's a magnificent horse, but I'm looking for a black one.
Donkeys are charming, but don't you have anything faster?

4.3.4 ADVISING

Why don't you take her to London?
You shouldn't eat so much/should eat less.
If I were you I'd ring the police.
You shouldn't have bought blue booties/should have bought pink ones.
If you want to save money you'd better spend less on your clothes.
You'll catch a cold if you don't get dressed.

4.3.5 COMPLAINING

Excuse me waiter, there's a squirrel on my table.
You might've warned him it was dangerous.
Why didn't you invite us to the wedding?
If I'd known why you wanted to borrow my car I'd never have
agreed.
You didn't tell me it was coming by donkey!

4.4 PERSONAL COMMENT

The language in the preceding sections has been controlled by the teacher, either by the form of his question about the picture, or by the form of the dialogue in which he has used the picture to prompt a response. It is also possible to stimulate uncontrolled responses from the students, by asking them to express their personal knowledge, experience or reactions with questions such as: *Who is this? What do you know about her? What meal is this? Is your breakfast the same? Where is this? Have you been there? Did you like it? Why? Is this what you do Sunday mornings? Why/Whynot? Has this ever happened to you? Tell us about it? What would you do if you saw a man in trouble like this? How would you feel if you saw a portrait behaving like this?*

To these questions, the students can choose their own replies. The form of the reply might be constrained by the limits of their fluency, or guided by structures you have been practising with them. The content of the reply, however, depends not on what you want them to say, but/or what they want to say. With interesting or controversial pictures this sort of personal comment can lead to general discussion, or even organised debate. Picture 23, for example, could lead to a general exchange of anecdotes and views about supernatural phenomena; Picture 1 could introduce the topic of occupational hazards, and lead to a debate on the responsibilities of employers.

5 Assembling Pictures

In some cases it is possible to derive a lot of classroom language from a single picture. We have seen, for example, how Picture 5 might be used to illustrate and practise several prepositional phrases. Picture 21 would be useful for teaching the vocabulary of family relationships: *husband, wife, father, mother-in-law, nephew,* etc. Picture 14 might be used to elicit several statements of prediction, and Picture 4 could be similarly used to elicit speculations about the crime that led to the man's arrest.

Usually, however, you will need several pictures for your classroom purposes; some of these will serve to introduce examples of the language you plan to teach, and others will serve as prompts for responses in practice drills. In this chapter you will find some advice on how to assemble sufficient appropriate pictures for your classroom needs.

5.1 PICTURES FOR SEQUENCE

When we are searching for picture sequences to use in the classroom, we think in terms of picture stories, like those shown in certain wallchart series, or in cartoon strips. These stories are useful for introducing and practising narrative forms. Magazine pictures cannot be connected to tell a story in this way. However, it is possible to put together certain pictures which will, in a context, form a logical or chronological sequence which will allow us to practise certain tenses, time phrases and sequence markers.

The present simple tense as used for habitual actions is commonly taught with reference to somebody's daily routine: *Every day he gets up, has breakfast, brushes his teeth, . . .* etc. Your library will not provide you with pictures of the same person doing all these things, but it will provide you with pictures which suggest these actions—a toothbrush, a plate of eggs, a pair of hands tying up shoelaces. Alternatively, you might decide to talk about a family routine: *First they have breakfast, then father goes to work, then mother does the washing; father has lunch in a restaurant; their son plays tennis every afternoon and his sister goes to a dancing class; in the evenings mother cooks the supper, the children wash the dishes, they all watch television . . .* etc. Or you might place the routine in an office context: *At 9 o'clock Mrs X opens the mail; at 10 Miss Y makes the coffee; at 11 Mr Z goes to the bank . . .* etc. Some of these statements can be illustrated with pictures from EVERYDAY ACTIVITIES but others can be equally well suggested with pictures from OBJECTS. The context and the way you order the pictures will supply the sequence.

Past tenses can be prompted with the same pictures, by changing the context:

> *What did he do yesterday?*
> *He got up, had breakfast, brushed his teeth . . .* etc.

With a little imagination, the context can be made more realistic:

> *I was trying to call the office all day yesterday. Where was everybody? I tried at 9.*
> *Mrs X was there at 9. She was opening the mail.*
> *Well she didn't answer the phone. Then I tried again at 10.*
> *Miss Y was there at 10. She was making the coffee.*

Students, too, can be asked to use their imagination to supply missing information. With a series of pictures from TRANSPORT you might prompt:

First he had a bicycle. He rode that until he was fifteen.
Then he got a motor cycle. He rode that until he got his first job.
Then he got an old car. He drove that until he got a pay rise.
Then he got a bigger car. He drove that until he inherited some
money.
Then he got a Rolls Royce ... a launch ... a jet ... etc.

Or to practise sequence markers you might ask students to choose a
meal from a selection of pictures from FOOD:

> *First I'll have some soup.*
> *Then I'll have some salad.*
> *After that... next... to follow... to finish...*

5.2   SETS OF PICTURES

While it is possible to assemble pictures in sequence, it is easier
to assemble them in sets which will be used to prompt alternative
responses or parallel responses. Pictures from FOOD AND
DRINK will cue substitutions in drills to practise questions with
some or *any*, or statements with *too much* or *too many, too little* or
too few. Pictures from OBJECTS will provide substitution items in
a wide variety of drills. Pictures from LOCATIONS might be used
to prompt questions in the simple situation: where's the cat?

> *Is it in the bedroom?*
> *Is it in the bathroom?*
> *Is it in the kitchen?... the garden?... the street?... etc.*

Pictures from RECREATIONS could be used to cue both question
and answer in a drill to practise gerunds.

> *Let's go swimming/fishing/cycling/climbing/skate-boarding.*
> *No thanks, I hate swimming/fishing/cycling ... etc.*

Pictures for a set need not be chosen from a single category. Examples of count and mass nouns, for instance, will be found in both FOOD and OBJECTS, and examples of gerunds can be elicited from EVERYDAY ACTIVITIES as well as from RECREATION. A set of luxurious things could be collected from categories such as BUILDINGS, OBJECTS, LOCATIONS, TRANSPORT and even FOOD AND DRINK to provide substitution items for the drill:

If I had the money I'd live in a palace/in Rome/in the tropics ... I'd buy a mink coat/a Rolls Royce/a yacht ... I'd eat caviare/drink champagne . . .

5.3   PICTURES IN COMBINATION

Sometimes you may want to prompt substitutions in two slots in a pattern. For this you may simply need alternative items from the same category, such as singular and plural items for:

We have plenty of Xs but there's only one Y left.

or contrasted items for:

He bought her a silver Z but she wanted a gold one.

or alternative activities for the responses such as:

While he watched television she washed her hair.
After she had washed her hair she watered the plants.

Picture combinations may be chosen from two different categories. For example, pictures from LOCATIONS and SITUATIONS could be chosen to form combinations to prompt some bad news along the lines of:

	in the garden	the cat ate the fish.
While you were	at the bank	somebody bumped into your car.
	at the market	the horses escaped.
	at the airport	your house burned down.

With picture combinations you can even ask the students to invent their own connections. Pictures 8 and 9 might elicit anything from the simple suggestions:

> *While he was walking to work he saw a white horse.*
> *He is happy because he is going to see his racehorse.*

to the more creative one:

> *He hopes it won't rain because he has lent his umbrella to his favourite horse!*

6 *Classroom Exploitation*

Magazine pictures, like all visual aids, will begin to bore your students if they are always used at the same stage of the lesson, in the same way, for the same purpose. Pictures may sometimes be your principal classroom aid, or they may be used to supplement other aids. Sometimes you will use them for a prolonged activity, and sometimes for a brief practice drill or review. Once you have mastered one way of introducing magazine pictures into your classes, you can experiment with others. Experience will familiarise not only you, but also your students, with the possibilities. You will soon find that conceiving, assembling and executing a classroom activity with pictures becomes second nature to you, and that your students will need no laborious explanations to know exactly what is required of them.

Chapter 3 gave some general advice on handling pictures in class. This chapter suggests some ideas for exploiting pictures at the presentation, practice and follow-up stages of your lessons.[3]

6.1 PRESENTATION

At this stage of a lesson the teacher's objective is to make the students aware of the *form, meaning* and *usage* of new language items.

The typical procedure for presenting a new oral *form* is to let the students hear a model. Some grammatical explanation may be made, either a simple one such as '*I've* is a contraction of *I have*' or a more complex one such as 'The present perfect passive is constructed with *to have + been + past participle*'. The students are familiarised first with how the model sounds (its phonological form) and later with how it appears (its orthographic form). Variants must be exemplified at some stage, so that the students will know how the form changes according to such factors as person (for example: *I have* but *he has*), negation (for example: *he has* becomes *he hasn't*), question (for example: *he has* becomes *has he?*) or intonation (for example: *Has he?* shows polite interest but *Has he!* can be disapproving).

Presentation of *meaning* was traditionally approached through translation, but the trend today, especially in multi-lingual classes where translation is not feasible, is to convey meaning through context. The linguistic context of new language items is largely familiar: thus new vocabulary may be presented in the context of familiar structures, or new structures in the context of familiar vocabulary. The situational context of new language items is presented in the form of a story or a dialogue which provides the student with clues he might use to deduce, or be helped to deduce, their meaning.

Usage is conveyed by making students aware of when, by whom, to whom and for what purpose the language is used. Thus, in the presentation of new language through dialogue, it is important that the students understand the nature of the situation, the identity of the speakers, their relationship, their mood, etc., and if the language being taught belongs specifically to one register, this should be made clear. It would be unfair, for example, to allow students to think that the way they have learned to invite a friend to a party would be appropriate for inviting a professor to speak at a meeting.

Pictures cannot help the teacher to present *form,* but they can be used to clarify *meaning* and, if used in an appropriate situational context, they can sometimes help the students to understand *usage.* They can, moreover, be used to help motivate students at the presentation stage of a lesson. You might exploit these possibilities in several different ways.

6.1.1 INTRODUCING TOPICS

Before presenting a story or dialogue it is sometimes helpful to establish the characters. For this you can choose suitable pictures from PEOPLE. You might tell the students their names, or you might ask students to choose these themselves. If it is relevant you might ask the students to provide more information about these characters, such as their age, or probable occupation, or you might ask them to establish some background by choosing from a selection of pictures an appropriate house, car, sport or even pet for each character.

When the new language is going to be presented in the context of information about a famous person, place or event, you can precede the presentation by showing an appropriate picture and eliciting whatever information the students can provide from their general knowledge. This technique serves not only to establish the topic, but also to activate known language. Thus we might precede the presentation of a text about the animated film industry by showing a picture of Mickey Mouse. From their general knowledge we would expect students to be able to associate *Walt Disney, Hollywood* and perhaps the date *1928*; from their existing vocabulary we might at the same time elicit *funny, character, drawing,* and perhaps *cartoon* or *fifty years old.* Then, when the students hear or read the text, they will be prepared to meet not only further facts about Mickey Mouse, but also new vocabulary such as *comical, animated* and *anniversary,* or such structures as *since 1928, for the past fifty years* or *fifty years ago.*

Pictures from SITUATIONS may also be exploited to introduce a topic. If the text is about an accident, or a robbery, or a stroke of good luck, a picture chosen to arouse preliminary discussion will set the students' expectations in the right direction. In this way pictures can be used to encourage students to recall what they know and make guesses about what they don't know before they are presented with a listening or a reading task.

6.1.2 PRESENTING STRUCTURES

Some pictures illustrate structures explicitly, and can therefore be used to clarify meaning. In JOBS, for example, pictures such as 15 can be found to illustrate the difference between the present simple and the present continuous tenses: *He is a chef. He cooks. He is not cooking now.* Among your DRINKS pictures you will find many showing bottles, cans, cups and glasses which could be used to present the present perfect passive form in statements such as *It has been opened.* Because the agent is not shown in these pictures the choice of the passive voice can be explained by asking: 'Can we see who opened it?', 'Do we know who opened it?', 'Is it better to say *Somebody has opened it* or *It has been opened*?', 'Why?'.

When presenting new structures in this way it is always helpful to establish what the students can say before teaching them what they can't. Thus, one might begin the presentation of a picture of milk bottles by asking: 'What can you see?', 'How many are there?', 'Are they all full?', 'How many are empty?', 'Why is it empty?' before presenting the model:

One bottle of milk has been drunk.

It is also important to decide in advance the stages by which you are going to introduce variant forms. When presenting the present perfect passive in this way, you would, for example, plan and assemble your pictures in the appropriate order to introduce, one by one, all the elements in the following frame:

It *One bottle* *One of the glasses* *A cup*	*has*			*opened.* *poured.*
		[not]	*been*	
They *Six bottles* *Two of the glasses* *All of the cups*	*have*			*drunk.* *emptied.*

To follow this presentation of *form* and *meaning* one might then assemble a set of pictures from other categories such as FOOD or OBJECTS with which to present *usage* in exchanges such as:

Are you hungry? Try some of this chicken.
  No thanks. It hasn't been cooked.
Would this bottle of perfume make a nice gift for mother?
  No it wouldn't. It's been opened.
Would you please exchange these shoes for me? They're too small.
  I'm sorry, I can't. They've been worn.
I didn't steal it, officer. Honestly, I've had it for years.
  What nonsense, it hasn't even been unwrapped!

6.1.3 SUPPLEMENTING OTHER AIDS

Presentation material is often designed in the form of spoken dialogue or printed text. Within these will occur vocabulary or structures which your students are to meet for the first time. If these are teaching points you will wish to spend time on them; if they are not, you may wish to pass over them quickly.

Preceding a dialogue or text with a list of new vocabulary items is not, in principle, a good policy. Students should be exposed to new language in context, so that they can learn to distinguish what they do understand from what they don't, and to make intelligent guesses based on linguistic and situational clues. However, it is helpful to prepare the students by helping to set their expectations in the right direction. One technique for preparing students to meet new vocabulary in a dialogue or text is to show pictures which illustrate the concept, and ask them to name it in any way they can. Thus Picture 14 could be used to elicit *talking*. Students can then be advised that they are about to encounter another way of saying *talking,* and after hearing the dialogue or reading the text some of them will be able to tell you the new word was *chatting*. Students may not always have a suitable word in their vocabulary to name what they see in the picture, but you can still prepare them to meet the concept. For example, before presenting a dialogue with the words *bride* and *groom* you might show Picture 21, saying 'We do have terms for a man and a woman on their wedding day, but I'm not going to tell you them now; see if you can tell me after you have heard the dialogue'.

Showing pictures to clarify meaning is of course not always possible. It would be very hard, for example, to use visual aids to illustrate the word *inflation* or the sentence *The crowd began to panic*. There are times, however, when a picture *can* be used to avoid laborious verbal explanation. It is much easier to explain what an English Christmas pudding is with a picture than with words. Similarly, the expression *fed up with* could be more efficiently explained with a picture of an exasperated driver in a traffic jam than with the linguistically complex explanation 'We say somebody is fed up with something when he has come to the end of his patience'. It is often possible to predict this kind of problem vocabulary and to have a suitable picture ready to show at the appropriate time.

Pictures can be produced after presentation of a dialogue or text to check understanding of new words. Don't, however, spoon-feed the students by simply saying 'This picture illustrates the meaning of the word *groom* in line 2'. First, review the passage and ask the students to identify unknown words. Then ask them to guess at their meaning. The pictures can then be used to confirm or correct these guesses. Alternatively you might show two or three similar pictures and ask the students to choose the one which best illustrates the meaning. Only one of Pictures 12 and 20, for example, could illustrate *having put on his shoes*.

6.2 PRACTICE

6.2.1 PROMPTING DRILL RESPONSES

At the practice stage of a lesson students are required to gain control of new language in spoken or written form. They may be practising recognition in listening or reading exercises, or they may be practising production in speaking or writing exercises. If the objective is mastery of oral production, then the students' task falls into three basic stages: (i) to get the form right, that is to choose the right words in the right grammatical form and to say them in the right order; (ii) to say them promptly, without hesitating or stumbling; and (iii) to pronounce them correctly, with correct stress, rhythm and intonation.

The traditional substitution drill was designed to give students oral practice of this kind. In these drills, students are required to manipulate a pattern sentence to include a substitution item. Simple substitution drills require the student to recognise the item, decide which slot it belongs in, and reproduce the pattern with the item in the correct place. More complex drills require students to substitute items in more than one slot, and to make the necessary grammatical changes according to number, gender etc.

Substitution drills have been criticised because they are mechanical and meaningless, and therefore give the students practice in nothing more than mimicry. It is, however, possible to design more effective drills by ensuring that the students know the meaning of what they are saying, by giving them a reason for saying it, and even, where possible, by adding an element of interest or humour in the hope that this helps them to enjoy saying it.

Pictures can be used in conjunction with verbal prompts to add meaning to student responses. In the following drill the substitution items would be *swimming, riding, fishing, cycling, climbing, skate-boarding*:

Stimulus: *Does Bill like —ing?*
Response: *No, he hates —ing.*

To be sure that your students are not just mechanically reproducing the cue word each time they respond, you might choose suitable pictures from your RECREATIONS file to illustrate these sports. By showing a picture each time you give a cue you can ensure, at least, that the students know the meaning of the word they are substituting in the pattern.

The same drill could be designed with a more appropriate stimulus, to give the students a reason for making the response:

Stimulus: *Will Bill come swimming with us next Sunday?*
Response: *I don't think so. He hates swimming.*

And by removing the verbal cue we can make the response dependent upon the picture, thus challenging the student to produce, rather than to copy, the correct substitution:

Stimulus: *Will Bill come with us next Sunday?*
Response: *I don't think so. He hates swimming.*

To make this drill more challenging, we might use pictures from LOCATIONS to cue *in the country, at the beach, in town, at home, at work, at the airport* to cue the first response in a two-part exchange:

Stimulus 1: *Where was Bill last Sunday?*
Response 1: *He was in the country.*
Stimulus 2: *We wanted to invite him to come with us.*
Response 2: *Oh, he wouldn't have come. He hates swimming.*

From this drill we might move to a personalised exchange:

Stimulus 1: *Where were you last Sunday?*
Response 1: *I was . . .*
Stimulus 2: *We wanted you to come out with us.*
             That was nice of you, but I hate ⎫
Response 2: *What a shame, I love*   ⎬ *—ing.*
                                                  ⎭

When designing a drill, it is important to think not only of how you might get the students to respond appropriately to your stimulus, but also of what reaction might be appropriate to their response. Thus, when using a picture to elicit questions such as *Have you looked in the . . . ?* you must remember to reply *Yes I have, and it's not there* before moving on to the next picture cue. Similarly, when asking students to suggest ways to help someone in trouble, such as the unfortunate signpainter in Picture 1, you should give some reason for rejecting each suggestion (such as *Well that's a good idea but the nearest telephone is ten miles away*) before asking for another.

Pictures may also give you ideas for humorous ways of practising well-worn structures. When faced with the problem of designing yet another drill to review comparative forms, for example, you might take pictures from the ANIMALS file to practise the pattern *what she wants is something a little—er* in the context of choosing a suitable pet for Grandma:

Stimulus: *Would this do?* (picture of an elephant)
Response: *No, what she wants is something a little smaller.*
Stimulus: *What about this?* (picture of a pig)
Response: *No, what she wants is something a little cleaner.*
Stimulus: *Well, this is a very clean animal.* (picture of a tiger)
Response: *No, what she wants is something a little tamer.*
Stimulus: *Tame. Hm. What about this then?* (picture of a rooster)
Response: *No, what she wants is something a little quieter.*
Stimulus: *Well, this is a very quiet animal.* (picture of a tortoise)
Response: *No, what she wants is something a little faster.*

Care should be taken to keep your pile of pictures face down, so that the students cannot see what is coming next until you are ready to reveal it. This is especially important when you have chosen your pictures especially to surprise the students in a drill such as the following:

Stimulus 1: *Where did you put the cheese?* (show picture of table)
Response 1: *I put it on the table.*
Stimulus 2: *You shouldn't have put it there. Look what happened.* (show Picture 23)
Response 2: *Oh! If I'd known that might happen I'd have put it somewhere else!*

6.2.2 GROUP OR PAIR PRACTICE

When a drill has been practised with the whole class, and the students are familiar not only with the language they are practising but also with the format of the drill, it is possible to set the same or similar drill for practice in groups or pairs. In this way you can multiply student talking time: instead of responding in chorus, or sharing the chance of an individual response with all the other members of the class, each student will be engaged in speaking to a partner, and in turn listening to his responses.

The procedure for introducing group or pair practice is important: students must understand precisely what is required of them so that they are not distracted from the purpose of improving their performance by doubts and misunderstandings. The teacher first presents the model exchange, then practises it with the whole class. He may make spot checks with individual students to establish whether they are able to form the response appropriately. The stimulus can then be provided by one half of the class, with the other half responding, and vice versa. Spot checks should be made again at this stage, to establish whether individual students are able to exchange stimulus and response. Any errors of performance should be carefully corrected while the teacher still leads the practice. Then, when the students seem to be aware of the standard they should aim for, they can break into groups or pairs to continue the drill, reversing roles from time to time.

In the design of drills for this type of practice it is necessary to control not only the response, but also the stimulus. In some drills the same picture can be used to cue both. In the following example, piles of small FOOD pictures in any order can be given to each group to cue both question and answer:

Student A: *Have we any . . . ?*
Student B: *Yes, we have one/some/a few/a little /a lot.*

In other drills the stimulus may take a standard form and only the response needs a cue. In the next example the students role-play a restaurant situation, and Student B chooses from the pile of pictures before making his response.

> Student A: *What would you like to order, sir?*
> Student B: *I'd like some soup.*
> Student A: *And then?*
> Student B: *I'd like a/some . . .* etc.

Drills which combine cues from two sets of pictures are difficult to cue with random piles. When you are controlling the practice, you can choose the combinations carefully to avoid producing nonsense such as:

> Stimulus: *I gave my brother a yacht for Christmas.*
> Response: *What a pity, he wanted a mink coat.*
>   or
> Response: *What a pity, he wanted a cigarette lighter.*

In groupwork, however, you cannot control the combinations which will result from random piles of pictures. It is therefore worth the extra effort to prepare a special file of 'connections cards' when you are assembling your library. Pairs of gifts, for drills such as the one above, can be pasted on to single cards so that they show appropriate alternatives for the same recipient. Other small OBJECTS can be paired to contrast size, or design, or number, in order to cue such exchanges as:

> Stimulus: *Do you like this chair?*
> Response: *I prefer that one. It's more modern.*

Other category combinations which are useful for 'connections cards' are LOCATION + OBJECT, LOCATION + PERSON, PERSON + TRANSPORT and JOB + RECREATION with which you might cue questions such as *Where does he keep . . . ? Where does he like to spend his holidays?, How does he get there?, What does he do on weekdays/at the weekend?* or more imaginatively constructed exchanges such as:

Stimulus: *Do you know X? He's the best... I know.*
Response: *Oh yes, I know him. I play... with him every weekend.*

For some types of group or pair work you can use big pictures from your file. Small pictures showing interesting SITUATIONS or INTERNATIONAL EVENTS will be hard to find, and in any case when these are needed for practice based on constructing imaginative explanations or recalling general knowledge, each group requires only one at a time, and can exchange. Famous BUILDINGS, LOCATIONS and even NAMES can often be found, however, on postcards, and these can be used to cue not only controlled questions such as *Where is... ?, What is the capital of... ?* and *Who is... ?,* but also free response to questions such as *Have you ever seen... ?, Would you like to go to... ?* and *What do you think of... ?*

There are also some published picture sets which can be added to your collection of small pictures for group or pair work.[4]

6.3   FURTHER ACTIVITIES

At some stage after presentation and practice, whether in the same or in a later lesson, students should be offered an opportunity to use newly-learned language in a different context, in a different activity, or for another purpose. If new language has been presented and practised orally, then a reading or writing activity may follow. Alternatively, after controlled practice the students will enjoy a game which calls on their newly-acquired skills. This final section suggests some ways in which magazine pictures can be used for follow-up activities.

6.3.1   READING AND WRITING

Some ideas for the preparation of individual workcards for reading and writing were mentioned in Chapter 2. Many pictures will serve either purpose—whether you add True/False statements or a short text for reading practice or questions or a gapped text for guided writing practice will depend on your needs and your inspiration.

The important factor in making a successful library of workcards is quantity. Each time you offer the class an opportunity to choose individual tasks for themselves you must have enough tasks at hand to occupy each student, or at least each pair of students. The range could include other materials of course, such as crossword puzzles or published readers, but you will still need to assemble several assorted pictures with reading and writing exercises of various kinds to practise language at specific stages of your syllabus.

Once you have collected sufficient tasks for the whole class you can, of course, keep the students busy on several occasions: when students complete one task they can exchange it for another. Meanwhile, until your library has grown, you can reserve your few workcards to occupy quicker students in class, or to offer to slower students for extra practice.

Reading and writing exercises can also be prepared to occupy the whole class. If your picture is large enough for all students to see, exercises such as those described on page 18 can be written on the blackboard, for students to answer individually or in groups. Groupwork composition tasks can also be set as a follow-up to exploitation and discussion of an interesting or topical picture. Students may be asked to write, for example, their own explanation and conclusion to the predicament of the signpainter in Picture 1, an insurance claim for the cost of repairs resulting from the accident in Picture 9, a report of the wedding in Picture 21 for the social column of a newspaper, or a letter to the 'Society for the Investigation of the Supernatural' about the phenomenon shown in Picture 23.

6.3.2 GAMES

Besides the student-access communication games described in Chapter 2, there are games which can be prepared with magazine pictures for playing by the whole class. Two of these can be compiled from your library files.[5]

Kim's Game is based on the memory training described in Kipling's famous novel, and is played with pictures from OBJECTS. A selection of pictures is laid out on a large table or on the floor and studied by all the students. Then each student chooses and conceals one. The object of the game is to collect all the pictures, but this can only be done by remembering who has which picture. In turn each student is given the opportunity to name a picture and request it from a specified player: *Michael, may I have the radio please?* If he has named Michael's picture he receives it; if he has not, the right to make a request passes to Michael, and so on until one student has collected all the pictures. This game can be played with selected pictures to practise vocabulary at any stage of the syllabus. The game can be made more complex by selecting pictures of similar objects which need a more detailed identification.

What is Common? can also be played at several levels, depending on the choice of pictures. This time the pictures are chosen from any category with one constraint: they must have one thing in common. The common element may be something concrete such as *glass,* something behavioural such as *eating,* or something abstract such as *poverty.* This time students see only their own picture, which is given to them by the teacher and concealed from the others. Questioning takes the form of *Is there . . . in your picture?* until one student can identify the common element. However, since no student wants to reveal prematurely the element he has in mind in case someone else guesses it first, the best questions are the most circumlocutionary ones. Students soon become practised at this technique, and play the game with increasing linguistic complexity.

The final game is of a type which can be prepared with duplicate sets of pictures. It is in fact a classroom version of *Describe and Arrange.* One example of this type is *The Furniture Shop.* Duplicate sets of pictures showing items of furniture are cut out of magazines and catalogues. One set is arranged and pasted on to a large card, on which has been sketched the interior of a room. The other set is pasted on to individual cards and a duplicate room is sketched on another large card. This game can be played as a competition between two teams. One team has the prepared furniture shop. The other has the shop and the separate furniture cards. Team 1 must tell Team 2 how to arrange the furniture cards to make an identical picture of the furniture shop, and the result is compared with the original. Since this game is dependent on both correct description and correct comprehension, mis-matches will lead to heated argument about whether it was Team 1 who described incorrectly, or Team 2 who misunderstood! Similar games can be prepared with pictures of cars in *The Parking Lot,* pictures of objects on *The Kitchen Shelf,* or pictures of people in *The Waiting Room*...your imagination will suggest many variations. You will find, moreover, that the linguistic level is not limited to elementary nouns, adjectives and prepositions of location. The language required to play these games is determined by the nature of the items and their arrangement on the frame, so the task of differentiating between the items and describing their position can be made more difficult. If you select very similar items, or increase their number, or make their arrangement more complex, you will be able to challenge even your most advanced students.

Preparing games such as these takes time, imagination and care, and you may at first prefer to content yourself with games which can be assembled from your library files. It is, however, a satisfying reward to see your students actively and fruitfully engaged in using language you have taught them to play a game you have painstakingly made for them. If this book has succeeded in persuading you to become an enthusiastic collector of magazine pictures as classroom aids, then it is only a matter of time, experience and inspiration before you will feel tempted to try these games and, undoubtedly, others of your own creation.

Notes

1 These games, and others, are described in greater detail in *Visual Aids for Classroom Interaction,* ed. Susan Holden, Modern English Publications, London 1978.

2 This important distinction was first made in 1963, in 'A theory of visual aids', English Language Teaching, Vol. 17, No. 2.

3 Some of these suggestions are demonstrated by Gill Sturtridge and Janet McAlpin in the British Council film, *Using Magazine Pictures in the Language Classroom* (1974). The film is available in the UK for hire and purchase from the National Audio Visual Aids Library.
Teachers in other countries should ask the local British Council representative for details about how to hire or purchase the film in their country.

4 *Picture Cue Cards for Oral Language Practice*, by J. Y. K. Kerr (Evans, 1979) is a further source of pictures and ideas for pair and group work. The kit consists of 300 laminated photographs and a teacher's handbook.

5 For *Kim's Game* and *What is Common?* I am indebted to Raymond Adlam of the British Council.

Teachers should further note that the originals of all the illustrations in this book were much larger and in colour. Size and colour are important factors in the appeal of these visual aids in the language classroom.

Pictures 1-24

Picture 1. From an advertisement for a newspaper

Picture 2. From an advertisement for chocolates

Picture 3. From an advertisement for life assurance policies

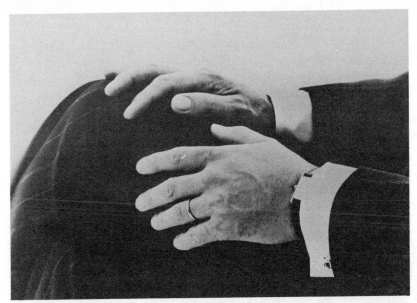
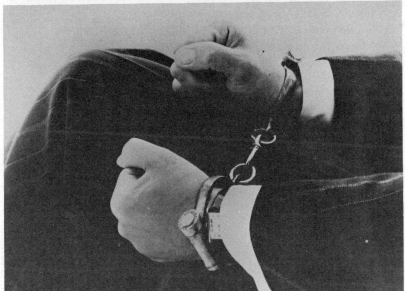
Picture 4. From an advertisement for industrial safety consultants

Picture 5. From an advertisement for a building company

Picture 6. From an advertisement for cigarettes

Picture 7. From an advertisement for insurance

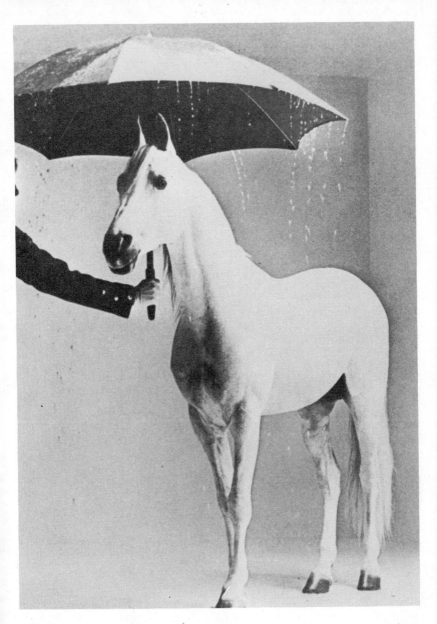

Picture 8. From an advertisement for whisky

Picture 9. From a greetings card

Picture 10. From an advertisement for coffee

Picture 11. From an advertisement for jewellery

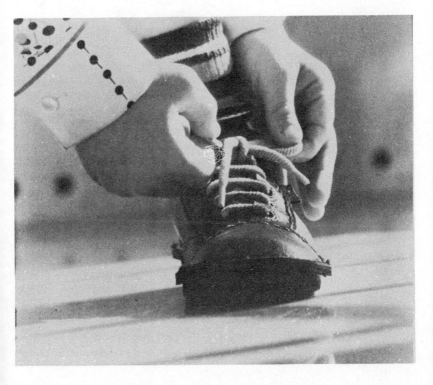

Picture 12. From an advertisement for the nursing profession

Picture 13. From an article on fruit

Picture 14. From an advertisement for central heating

Picture 15. From an advertisement for champagne

Picture 16. From a publication about the 1977 Jubilee celebrations in Britain

Picture 17. From an article on the Trooping the Colour Ceremony

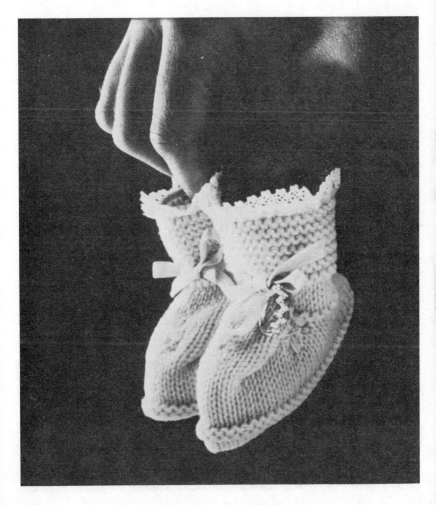

Picture 18. From an advertisement for diamonds

Picture 19. From an advertisement for men's clothing

Picture 20. From an advertisement for footwear

Will success spoil Harry Taylor?

Harry Taylor would have made it anyway. (Didn't his mother always say so?) Marrying the boss's daughter was just a happy accident.

So there won't be too many changes in Harry. After all, there are some things in this world you just can't improve on. Even if you tried.

Like the Scotch you drink.

Johnnie Walker — the smooth one.

But then, it's only natural that the world's most successful Scotch whisky should be the drink of the world's most successful men.

Men like Harry Taylor?

Stop fooling around, choose **Johnnie Walker** — we make it for people who've made it.

Picture 21. From an advertisement for whisky

Picture 22. From an advertisement for a car

Picture 23. From an advertisement for cheese

Picture 24. From an article on Mexico

Index of References to Pictures